body & *field*

body & *field*

Poems *by*
Terry Blackhawk

[handwritten inscription:]
Terry Blackhawk

For Beth Gylys —
Sister poet! With
warmest wishes —
peace & joy —

Terry

Michigan State University Press
East Lansing

∞ The paper used in this publication meets the minimum requirements of
ANSI/NISO Z39.48-1992 (R 1997) (Permanence of Paper).

Michigan State University Press
East Lansing, Michigan 48823-5202

03 02 01 00 99   1 2 3 4 5

Library of Congress Cataloging-in-Publication Data

Blackhawk, Terry, 1945-
    Body & field / Terry Blackhawk.
        p.   cm.
    ISBN 0-87013-518-X (alk. paper)
    I. Title. II. Title: Body and field
    PS3552.L34235 B63 1999
    811'.54—dc21   99-6089
                                                                          CIP

Lotus Poetry Series Editor: Naomi Long Madgett
Book and Cover Design by Michael J. Brooks
Cover photo by Heather Elton, courtesy of the Banff Centre
    for the Arts

Visit Michigan State University Press on the World-Wide Web
www.msu.edu/unit/msupress

for Evan

Contents

iii.
Impressionable Earth

iv.
The Work of Her Hands

v.
Clearing the Bird

Acknowledgments

Grateful acknowledgment is made to the editors of the magazines in which the following poems first appeared: "The Syrian Boys" (as "Commencement") in *America;* "Waterworks" in *College English;* "Learning to Ride English" in *Cranbrook Review;* "At Silver Creek Presbyterian Church" in *The Driftwood Review;* "At the Raku Firing" in *Garfield Lake Review;* "How Eagerly This Humid Night" in *Iris: a Journal about Women;* "The Dawn of the Navajo Woman" in *The Louisville Review;* "At the Moscow Circus," "Blanket," "The Blues, 'The Bay,'" "The Dream" (from "Commencement"), "Leda," and "Letter Perfect" from *The MacGuffin;* "On the Mockingbird Singing in the Morning in the Barrio a Few Blocks from the Boardwalk on the Beach in Venice, California" in *the Marlboro Review;* "February Teacher" in *Passages North;* "Voyager" in *Poet Lore;* "And Where Were the Foxes?" in *River Oak Review;* "Reader Response" in *The Comstock Review;* "Penelope, Taking Stock" and "Still Life with Migraine" in *The Sow's Ear;* and "Calling the Owl" and "On Hearing the Songs of Wolves as Mirrors of Desire" in *Yankee.* "Memorial Day Weekend" and "Anasazi Bowl" were included in *Still Life with Conversation: Poems from the Stage Production,* Rebecca Emlinger Roberts (ed), Ridgeway Press, 1993. "Examining the Heat Exchange Over a Mug of Tea" appeared in *I Am Becoming the Woman I've Wanted,* Sandra Martz (ed), Papier Mache Press, 1994. "Pasiphae: What She Wanted" was included in *Trio: Voices from the Myths,* Ridgeway Press, 1998.

The author wishes to express her gratitude to the Michigan Council for Arts and Cultural Affairs for an Artist-in-the-Schools grant during the time when this manuscript was completed. Grateful thanks also to Elizabeth Socolow, Bill and Judy Michaels, Bill Harris, Naomi Long Madgett and Patricia Hooper for their help with this collection of poems.

The Music in the Violin
Does not emerge alone
But Arm in Arm with Touch, yet Touch
Alone—is not a Tune—

Emily Dickinson

i.
Bloodrush

The Dawn of the Navajo Woman

(for Evan)

The Navajo medicine woman gets up early
to greet the sun. So my radio tells me
and so I stay tuned, though you already showed
the way of greeting: simply to hold
this winter the hickory nut brushed free
of snow, the plain prize beneath the season's tree.

Perhaps it's the way your arch fits my instep,
my instep curves over your arch, but we've kept
at it these years, our limbs linking and unlinking deep
in the quilting, and still a hunger for skin, not sleep,
leads me on to you, your hand on my breast or
your calm talk of death and the ghosts of our ancestors,

all of them gone into the crowded earth. Such
comfort and ease I can almost consider becoming mulch
myself. Or ash. And I wonder at how a rush of heat can
disperse into something so much bigger than I am
that it leaves me pulsing, ignoring what's beyond,
daring to dispute the frozen ground.

The predawn sky offers an arctic green
below a blanket of flaming clouds. I try to imagine
the devotions of that Navajo woman but get only as far
as yesterday when we detoured through a graveyard
seeking, after shopping, a more quiet crowd.
The sun dazzled us: stark trunks thrusting upward

in the polar air, a batch of mallards in a bubbled
pool and all around the bright untroubled
snow. In the granite names I read the luck and rhythm
of even this hair's-breadth of a life, your breath with mine,
the branches swirling by, and the bobbing ducks, their
emerald heads flashing a green and palpable fire.

At the Raku Firing

beside a makeshift kiln,
we circle one another, waiting
for the incandescent forms
to be pulled with tongs, birthed
like that, into open air.

A late September moon marks time
through the beech tree's brittle leaves
and each pot brought forth is a molten moon,
a source of sudden combustion
to be smothered in sawdust or woodchips
that burst into smoke and flame.

Later, with woodsmoke lacing my clothes,
I come home, hand him the newmade bowl,
and he, drawn by moonlight, steps outside, alone.
I go to bed, am tired, have already been
out in the moon—and when he returns,
with his moon-cool touch, at first
I say I don't want him: sleep
seems more luscious than sex—
but something about the bowl—
the way I glazed and drew it glowing
from the kiln, crouched there
and hoped for the colors to turn,
the outer wall iridescent,
the interior crackled, white,
with dark lines holding the smoke—

there's a moon in the bowl, white
in the well and I am a well
I am looking down into
moonlight reflected, contained
in a glaze selected
from vats of possibility:

the wrist swirls quickly,
fingers holding the bowl
by the bottom—a swift twist
coats the inner surfaces.

Who knows what fire will do?

I'm lucky, get what I want—
that violet sheen,
those greens and red—fiery, metallic.

Examining the Heat Exchange
Over a Mug of Tea

Soon you will re-enter
this room. You will be showered,
shaved, zipped. But for now

a fractal warmth fills
my porcelain cup, fills my touch,
my skin's minutest whorls.

Reddening capillaries
activate god knows what
goddess within:

my sweet depths where
you lose yourself,
our gasps, the glow

of your skin against mine.
Where do we go then
only to return, dazed,

mussed, and set dreamily
musing, so permeable
to light passing through

these reversible blinds
I can barely reassemble myself
to sit here, to hold, trace,

infer with my pattern of prints,
this patterned, heat-bearing
wall? Oh, soft, most flexible pads,

enabling me to be known,
and to know—radiance
from a mug of tea!—

and the way blood carries
messages, crosses pulse
points, oxygenates itself

so that even at my fingertips
I sense my transpiring
breath, but feel no sweat, nothing

remarkable, just everyday touch,
I/you, the warmth only our bodies
can teach us, this throbbing

reaching out, this hunger
not to be alone in our
unremarkable hearts.

Straight Ahead and Over Easy

Weekend mornings blessings abound
though last night's rainy road
was less certain as I stuck
to that trucker's slipstream, following
his tailgate square, despite fog,
sleep edging in, and managed
a steady pace, glad for the guidance,
the strong arm at the wheel.

Now in this John Deere diner
with its truckers, maleness *en masse*,
I follow you into the story you retell,
the one about the runaway's lost mother,
how he swore he'd recognize her the moment
he saw her, then sat next to her a quarter hour,
fidgeting in front of the judge
without knowing who she was.

Or his fistfight, in hospital,
with the demented woman in the green
ballgown. But it's your story,
not mine. I'm not that greenclad woman
or mother on the lam. Delicate
banter, minor matter. And, no,
I won't be wearing your ashes
in a deerskin bag around my neck.

And you won't plant me.
Testaments can take tricky turns:
we never know when we'll need to
downshift, slip into reverse,
back up off the on ramp into
oncoming traffic in the dark,
then come home grateful to be able
to tell it at all. So, yes,

these eggs and sticky buns may subtract
several hours from the nether end
of our days, but our weekend travels,
this breakfast and the rain make me
plainly happy, like the stories
we keep turning to, renewing old
delight, retreading familiar paths,
listening well, getting it right.

Dancing with My Son

Every body's doing it, this downright
boogie-down hustle and twist. We're trout
responding to a built-in magnetism,

some homing sense that sends us
leaping up ladders against the falling
water. Were we born to this?

When I ask my son how he learned
to dance so well, he says
it's in the genes, that pool

that pulls us in to this swirl
of couples on the floor. The deejay
alternates reggae thumps

with a swept-away sentimentality.
It's Elvis and we're all fools
rushing in under the predictable

mirrored ball. Someone waves
a wand of bubbles. My friend says,
"He was supposed to marry me"

as her son dances with his bride.
I won't catch the bouquet.
I am joined in a new union

of mother-son—he as surprised
as I, though there's no uncertainty:
just his fragrance, his shirt,

his broad-shouldered, slow-
stepping grace. He enters a world
I think he'll master—and I'm part of it,

this primordial room, its surge
of arms, bodies, flow. It's the sea
and I can't help falling, we're under

water, creatures who bob through tides
of rhythm and light. We're Y, M, C, A-ing
loosening ties, losing inhibitions,

until I'm rising, lucky as a balloon
with my new partner who knows
exactly when to let the string go.

Blanket

You hold the flimsy blanket
as if it were a relic,
this worn square you found,
stuck in some crevice
when you rearranged the closet wall
to look for a leak in the plumbing.
So this, I think, is how we treat
our treasures—this one,
old as our son, or surely older,
even if we count
his months of gestation.
It had a satiny edge then,
but now the fuzz is gone
and I can see through it
where the threads cross
like lace or netting,
leaving room for air.

You've made a point
to show me this. Deetee,
you say, and I repeat,
deetee, though how he
got to there from "blanket"
I'll never know. His code
for comfort, his first invented
word. For my brother,
it was bockey. Munga, to his son.
And here we repeat: deetee,
deetee. But I think put it back,
oh, put it back. I'll not see it
out like this, useless in your hands.
Save it for the long season.
Put it back with the rattling crib,
the sweaty head nuzzled
to my lips, the sweet salt.

Find some better storage,
dark and warm, where it can pulse
and leak and whisper and release for us
that necessary rhythm, those soft
sufficient syllables: munga, bockey,
heartbeat, bloodrush   deetee
deetee deetee

Commencement

i. The Syrian Boys

Like the boys I once saw in Homs
flinging themselves from the topmost
turn of a Roman waterwheel—

their arms and legs wildly akimbo,
caterwauling, graceless,
yet full of a coltish grace—

my son casts his eyes to the ceiling,
speculates about the plants, wolfs
his food, restless, ready to reach

the top of this one wheel's turning,
his first outward launching
making him nervous, skittery

unwilling to answer even the most
direct question. How the waterwheel
must have creaked and groaned then,

beneath those Syrian boys.
It was amazing, a monument
turned plaything. Over and over

they climbed and sailed out, shrieking
through the bright air, catching the turns
just so, spilling with the water

but disdaining for the moment
its gravity. Circumscribed
by today, and less a parent

than a tourist in a dusty land,
I'm amazed to think of those boys
as I watch him finding his foothold

nearing the apogee, asking nothing,
poised above the pool, casting about
for the finest way down.

ii. *The Dream*

When cars pass, the pavement hisses.
Her son will not return this evening but she
does not stare into the night. No,

she sleeps, her limbs thickened
with sleep. And she sweeps. In her dreams
she is sweeping, stirring corners overflowing

with breezes from her uncurtained
windows. Sometimes she thinks she moves
only air, but she does not stop.

At the foot of her bed is a child
who needs a specific thing, who stands quietly
in his quilted snowsuit.

Who is he? What does he want from her?
Things need returning to their proper
places. She has given herself this task

and so moves dispassionately, retrieving
wandered nestlings, kittens no larger
than her palm. She knows order

is best uncovered in the looking *for*:
not like this, this putting away.
But here she is, picking up things.

Now she holds a four-footed figure, its clay
not quite dry, like cool leather in her hand.
But mostly she puts back the small ones,

plump and warm. Even if they stray
she will find them. The piglets, together
thanks to her, suckle at last in a line

by the door, the lost one snugly in place,
the great sow's back rising and falling
over her indistinguishable young.

iii. Departure

On the poster you left behind,
a child in dark glasses sits and swings
her feet in a gutter, a smiling,

defiant gum-chewer, an angelic twist
to her lips. I pass her, calm and dry-eyed,
moving through this latest emptiness,

straightening last year's ties,
your out-worn shoes, eighteen years
passed so soon. Each spring's roses

mark your birth. Some say the earth
gives us messages and I half
believe it, though what I've given you

I cannot tell. How closed you tried
to be with me. The more I worked to warn you,
the louder my parental flutterings

became, the less you wanted to hear.
You grew your own way and then you were gone,
your absence shimmering behind you,

almost a solid thing, touchstone
to my tenderness. So when you called
to ask for cash—your outstretched palm!—

I thought I was over the worst, felt relieved
to recover the known—the comic,
the usual irritations. Yet how to align

this longing with my seeming normalcy?
The dailiest gestures unfold
to memory and I am not surprised

at what I find: you, opening, everywhere.
The wheel turns. How can I explain this
holding, this fine emptiness, this full heart?

How Eagerly This Humid Night

Your flashlight beam leaps along the trunk
as we stand barefoot on the lawn and watch
baby raccoons emerge the first time this spring.

They chir to each other and their nails scrabble
down the old maple. Already I'm older.
I say "such a racket," then regret it.

Our son has moved into his own sphere
yet something still carves along my spine,
expanding my ribs the way roses spilled

over fences that time of full burden
when each inhalation brought a strength like bark,
a solid inner breath. Despite storms,

the tree stays. Major limbs torn like paper.
The honeybees it housed have not returned.
These lingering evenings I think

we'd best not try to fill our silences.
The glancing leaves signal me, aimlessly,
like words. I want to tell you, though.

I want to say *bark, trunk, mouth-pressed*. I think
viscera, mossy earth and how twenty years ago
you painted our room the color of the sky.

We climbed the simple steps and I thought
I knew the hour we conceived. Sore breasts,
the first sign. It was November by then,

the slow notes rising, the time it took
to learn the beauty of carriage,
so as that summer opened around us

and moths spun stars in the lamplight
I would swell and sail forward, helpless
to do otherwise than let my largesse lead us.

I am filled now with the green ink of evening
and you, the words I do not use
to part and spell our undiminished air.

ii.

Prehistoric Beasts

The Birth

i.

A heavy beast plodded through me,
the hooves leaving imprints
outside and in. The huge muzzle
browsed my ear and when I did not scream
breathed sibilant blessings.
My breasts throbbed. I paced and paced.
It did no good. Wherever I went, the animal
went also, a four-footed shadow.
It was as if I trod on swampy ground.
But I myself was tender earth, a membrane,
a wall, the side of a stall
the calf's head butted and butted.
Who or what would be
mattered less than the sweat
pouring from my brow like wax overflowing,
the endless waiting, contractions.
How eagerly I stared at that mirage
of parrots, bright flashes,
the macaw almost in flames.
But I was not fire. I was wet,
drenched, holding for dear life
to my mother's hand. I thought
the being I carried would reflect
all the colors I knew, but the relentless
pushing blinded me and I guessed then
what she would become, my difficult one.
I did not release or let her go but held on
and stared into a glaring white intensity.
All I saw was the sun as she went out of me,
fierce and kicking, awash into the world.

ii.

Difficult? No, delicate—
the way I am walking
through newly moist air.
Dust fills the corners
of my mouth. Dry tongue, dry teeth
but the light suggests an early spring,
ivy asserting its bitterness.
I am not far from her garden,
my mother who comes from a dry land and winds
that speak of anger and promises
she will never mention. I wonder
what is in that box
she keeps locked beneath the stair.
But I am walking. This is the new season,
bloom of water spraying lawns in the late evening.
Light rushes through me. I am full
of curtains and whispers and this child
who will fly—escape on her wing.
She will be a girl, this innocent of veils.
She will be a swan, a flower on pointed toes,
so poised we will weep at her fluttering
dress, the exquisite arch of her neck.
Her feet punctuate my breath. The hallway swirls
around me the way the sidewalk
ribboned to the wide room
where we learned to circle following
the leader, how to alternate, skip
on the other leg, lift
the other foot. I was flexible then
but now my feet are flat
and I am heavier
and lighter than ever before.

iii.

Who enclosed this jungle here, flowers
flashing the atrium? When I look up, I see mountains
and the sun rocking
like a horse in his silence. I am rocking
like the sun. I am rocking
like the garden. Huge lilies
unfurl, thrust upward.
When she arrives, she will
twirl them like parasols.
She rides now, suspended in her basket,
ready to fill the hole in the curtain
that light bleeds through, like time.

Tarantella

Odd awakening, my childish body
recoiled on the bed as my foot reached
and found her, the mother wolf-spider
who had chosen that morning

to fill my innocent shoe. Though I'd best
not call it choosing. Our partners
may be spun in set designs long before
the dance we're bidden to begins.

How many was she? Hundreds, disturbed
more by my foot than my scream
as I drew back and shrieked, grabbing
sheets around me, staring in sheer

disbelief at the live birth, the dark
pulsing shapes, the tiny orgasmic
beings jarred from her hairy back,
swarming up the spread.

I've learned since not to deny the spinner
her glistening, dark-born dreams,
but then the maternal body
seemed a wide, obnoxious eye.

And my own shoe, the source of such vision!
What to do but follow that lead:
not my father's, whose can of spray
would rescue me from the rising forms—

but that opening nod from an untamable world
I would step forward forever barefoot into.

Hints of Betrayal

Twelve. It rained
that entire week we spent in Fort Lauderdale.
I played solitaire on the breezeway,
caught frogs by the handful, weighed under
by the humid air.

Today's radio tells me the season
has opened on alligators, but after three weeks
of being nailed by floodlights
the prehistoric beasts are getting wary.
I love hearing how their eyes glow pink
as beams sweep the water's surface
before they flick their enormous tails
and disappear. I don't know what to do
with the news you've given me.

When we vacationed at nine
the Smokies were arid, the water there
held back by a massive dam. I rode
the ponies alone. You spent that week
bedridden with hives, turning over
an occasional jigsaw or card.

Now I rearrange old games
and diversions, brushing back cobwebs
from shelves disordered and dry.
You have kept it so long,
this piece you hold out to me,
my old king. Will it help if I take it
and put it away, this piece of a puzzle
I didn't know I was missing?

Green and Red

If petals could be currency, I was the thief
of bloom. I tried to replant the stolen stems
then hid beneath the red-checked cloth
when winter came to get me. If I closed
my eyes when air turned cold, the world
disappeared to red.

Near a rock wall an old man showed me flowers
with fuzzy green petals. Daddy
ate watermelon. It was red, too.
I wanted to discover how red I could be
so I sat on the couch and gazed
at my hands. Books weren't red
but they could be decorated. I covered
the flyleaf with triangles and squares
but they had no magic in them.

If I swallowed a coin perhaps I would be
worth counting. Pennies were almost red.
I put one under my tongue
and climbed to that stair halfway up
where I could come to almost any conclusion.
The penny was simply an accident,
thus no accident at all, but a third woman
knew what to do about it and nursed me through.

If my father took me to see a famous ship
and then to the theater and then to the sea
where the ocean clanged through the night, all this
was green, not red. The sky was green and the sea
was green. The white walkways of the ship
were edged with green and when we were rained on
in the park we stood under a green-leafed tree.

My shoes were red. He retrieved them from the children
who stole them from me and brought them home
through the green evening. I was lonely then.
I opened the door and found a red fringe
of flowers and a bee
bumping across each bloom.
I was not born in that garden.
But now I think the first green is red.
I see it in the buds of the maple,
the earliest color in spring.

Pegasus

It's a hot afternoon. I am running
        naked across the lawn, wearing nothing
                but panties, laughing
          through curtains of spray, trying to leap over them,
              to become

a horse with wings like the red silhouette
        on the gas station sign, arms wild and out—
                then to come down
         to earth, nose pressed close, to force my cupped
hand
                over the stream.

I smell the green of my grandmother's lawn,
        bitter pearly leaves, not grass exactly, but tiny points
              soaked like a sponge.
         I make a fist, squish, squeeze. Now I squat, straddle
             the sprinkler, let the surge

soak into my white cotton crotch. I am delicious,
      I am five, or three. I spread my legs closer to
            the hiss. Am I noticed here
        between the porticoed porch and the palm tree where
          I know the moon

nests among dates at the top of the trunk?
        Next summer I will play statues on this lawn, freeze
            into awkward shapes, fling, rush,
       hurl, then stop, arrested. Now water waves like a
fan.
             I am on the edge

of shimmer, of possessing the sheen I run through.
       I crouch over the flow, let it push into a tingly twirl
             like the umbrella plants I pluck

30

then spin, dried lacy parasols. But this is a wet
                              swirl. I guess I know
it's forbidden. Oh, the laugh rises, the bubble loosens
          in my throat. I am shrieking, I am hilarious, head
tossed,
                              hair flying. Whose hand
            turns the spigot, opens the burble, sop, shush
                    of water and lawns,

                    releases this spray in the evening
                        the stone sky closes down?

31

On the Warmth of Horses

Perhaps it was to tame
the ancient horse and prevent fiery hooves from opening
the ground to bear off one more innocent
daughter that the neutering began.

Or the way the daughters
watched the horses, imagined being carried
straddled naked against velvet hide—
dreamed interstellar journeys, asserting themselves
into glimmering space, where it was always
a horse carried them, carried her.

She was skinny, eight or ten, and the way she regarded
the animal confirmed what the father already saw—
how she would take in her teeth whatever rope she could find,
toss her head, whinny to girlfriends
who tossed manes in reply, stamp,
flare nostrils, stretch out a tentative palm
to the curious padded muzzle
whuffing hot breath on her hand.

Not the rough tongue,
it was the lightest touch she loved,
delicate, delicate—the taking
with flexible lips a slice of fruit or carrot
into the meditative mouth.

Cold evenings she sought the warmth
of horses, leaned over the slatted stall
and the father found her standing there
distracted, watching.

Learning to Ride English

If I did not press my thighs hard
against his sides, my legs would flop
and she would yell, "I see daylight!"

I often wondered what she saw,
with mostly horse between my legs,
but I obeyed. "Post! Don't bounce!"

Move with the animal. Although she never
said it like that: *with the animal.*
Even now muscles remember—how to rise

piston-like against the trot, or pull
his head right, then squeeze and rock forward
into his forelegs' gallopy reach.

At the far turn, around the barn,
a deep green shade extended
to the creek, coolness

seeping in from the cave beyond.
There I would gather myself
before emerging again to her scrutiny.

Dismounting meant turning the stirrup,
chest stretched against unyielding
leather, trembling legs descending.

I was her last lesson before we moved
toward evening, soaping tack, feeding,
putting away, the contented jowls munching.

And this was my first love, not the boy
whose silvery smile I barricaded my bedroom
door against, the one who would kiss me,

later, but the beast a woman taught me to ride
her voice and eye following me
from the center of the ring.

Little Red

Imagine her not hooded or coy.
No inadvertent blush
to stamp her victim forever.
But let us take her
as she was in the old story
having chosen the path of needles
over the path of pins.
Not a child, no father ahead
or mother behind
to frame her journey with admonition
or reward. None of this
prettification, simpering
rosepetal baskets or little feet,
but a child-woman on the verge
of learning her own utility,
how to resist, be strong.
Needles, not pins.
Wit will be her weapon,
and flesh—so when she lies
naked next to the wolf, even there
bawdiness will save her
and she will tell him
she needs to dump a load.
How can he argue the body's truth?
What to do but wait and say go?
Imagine the darkness, the orchard
outside Grandmother's cabin,
fruit trees clouding above her
as she slips free of his bonds,
escapes into the apple-cool night,
and leaves him lying there, slathering,
stupid and confused, pulling
the rope he tied her to, finding it limp
in his hands.

Leda

All day long I twisted
and turned
like a cat in heat
so my prayers were easy
and I was not surprised
at how quickly he came
with his hissing glide
across the smooth waters.
It was a sight all right—
the arc of his wing,
that snaking neck—
but there was no trick to it.
I always knew he'd pick
me, glib mortal
girl, target
for his flimsy passion.

How he flashed and preened.
It was laughable really,
that self-importance,
those ludicrous pinions
beating the air around me.
He was strong,
but I held him, breast
buttock and thigh
before brushing off
the sweat-stained feathers.
What these gods wouldn't give
for some solid flesh.

But still, I liked
his costume and anyway
it wasn't half bad
for a small devotion.

Penelope, Taking Stock

Arachne was a wild thing then, not one
to settle down. I'd watch her
stuffing garments into her knapsack.
Once she got the urge to go
there was no stopping her.
She always told me not to make
too much of my patterns. But I
couldn't help it. How I loved
my Limoges, my Reed and Barton.
How honored at my reception:
the smiles all around sparkled
and buoyed me into life with you.
Such riches. So well planned.
At night I'd peek into the drawers
or flick the crystal's rim
just to hear it ring, before turning down
our crisp, clean sheets.

I waited, eagerly at first. But you
needed other satisfactions. Fishing.
Bow-hunting. Hopping from one remote
island to the next. I know what goes on
in those god-forsaken little trailers
parked in the scrubby woods. The sleazy
women, those sows from the city. And
the look in your eye, bleary, debauched,
oh mighty hunter, when you return
with the deer strapped to your fender.
And now you sit there as if nothing
has happened? Well, twenty years
amortize strangely, don't they?
Your son barely knows you. You're
turning to fat, while here in the kitchen,
I, who have nothing but my hands, I
polish and order, I sharpen the knives.

Birthing the Minotaur

(after Jackson Pollock's "Pasiphae")

She is being pulled apart.
The elbow dissociates itself.
Ribs, carpals, clavicle
take leave of her, cleaving the air
like a flock of crows, each bone's
a new dark flapping thing.
She watches them ascend to the cciling,
exit the window and scatter like flags
getting caught in the trees—these bones, flip side
of her being, shadows that have risen
and gone on without her. And what's left
are not the hysterical distal joints
but stubborn, solid—skull and pelvis,
pelvis that will not cease
its chatter and rattle. Rattle of tooth
and jaw. Shiver of heat and cold.
She's a skull she thinks she's a mind
absorbed in lust. The push
within her is not glistening wet,
but a dry birth, hooved and horned,
just as she's become bone,
stretched across this desert. She's
a window, she looks into and through
herself: her hipbones
are huge—aching temples, empty
frameworks, eye-sockets,
hip-sockets, nothing in them but eyes,
all eyes now, looking down her through her
canal of days.

Pasiphae: What She Wanted

—What She Wanted

I wanted to be the sun and the moon
framed in the same window.

I thought I could land forever
on my feet, thought whatever tide
tumbled and pummeled me would thrust me
upright at last on solid ground.

I had no idea edges
could blur so completely, wishes
change to curses and the seed of no return
fasten in my womb.

Beast, yes, though the god could have sent me
anything—a frog, a duck—so bored I'd become
with the king and his self-
anointed ways, years of the same endless slap

of waves against our shore. And if I was
water-witched, it was not water I wanted
but its massive manifestation, surge made solid,
all that briny spume and foam turned flesh,

the mountainous might and hulk of him.
I wanted to cry out shrilly.

No mere ox could ease the sorcery.
No woodland song dispel
what seeps from the corner of the eye.

It set me nights wandering
our moonlit grounds, the earth
cindery as spent lava beneath my feet.

—*She Walks Along Low Tide at Sunset*

In the foam's amber wash
she marks cessations of desire,

mistakes bird's foot for crab-
trace against the trembling sand.

The hour hands her its shadow,
so stunning an inversion it seems

she's let decades go by
determining the precise role

of the wave, fish scales that flash
like minuscule coins, or eyes.

No music now, no trumpets,
moans. Just the surf's insinuating

sighs. And if watchers spread tales,
what of it? She's settled in

for her aftermath, here where breath
arrives on behalf of this bronze-

edged slant as she succumbs
each day to the dropped sun

cascading down the ladder
at the end of the world.

—Salt

No pity.

I tried to go beyond the extremes,
but all I learned was not to lean
too far into corners. I'm good now
at pretending I don't hear my name
wound around knife-thin whispers.

These days tenderness no longer
feels like tinder. I've forgotten
how to flash, then flare.
If only I could find that fire
I'd hurl words essential as salt

against these wretched walls.

—Pasiphae Sees a Light Which Has No Obvious Source

Let the earth open, I thought.
I could be a wife with a fish's tail.
I could be a woman in a frame playing tricks
on a bull. From my garden by the sea,
I watched the setting sun
while beneath the lily at my feet a light
started to gleam. I was over forty by then
and still these possibilities. A square
of gold on the earth. Light coming at me
from behind. The air suggested mind and its hungers—
how in truth it was not body impelled me,
but thought, idea, the notion of knowing that being
with my skin, the way the creature breathed.

I could be blind, I thought. I could have invented this world.

—She Considers the Approach of Winter

So, summer,
you've gone that same way we'd swirl twirl ourselves,
sweet sex and all that verbing up in smoke, the sticky bed
I stumbled from, and the earth, I swear I went beneath it—
below that pasture holding two of us who were not
two to speak of, but the thrust of one will, one trouble, my
candle that gutters in the dark. Yet still the fields reveal
themselves beneath shocks of grain. I remember rattles,
blades in the wind, a raspy hush that persists even at higher
elevations where partridges leave tracks in the snow.

—Making Way

Nightfall she crosses
headlands by the sea, making way
for a daughter who's already gone.

Boats dot the waters.
A voice calls out *we've been here before.*
She sees the phosphorescent

wake, starry specks,
the whole reeking slightly
of dried puffers, blowfish.

With a less generous heart
she might not fill with tenderness.
She could be a prow

cutting the waves, a sieve
to retrieve what the years
furrowed through her flesh.

42

—Pasiphae and the Bees

Fingers somewhat stiff these days.
I hear bees working and wonder
if bees are enough to repair the world's dark
twanging strings. Why do I remember it
all as yellow, the meadow filled
with asters and the sea not far away?

Two ancient apple trees grew nearby.
If he had been able to speak,
if he had been able to speak . . .
but there was only the trumpeted rush
of breath and behind that the drone
of bees, an ocean of pollen,
grasses, grain—and me immersed,
so pounded, wave upon wave,
I seemed to fall below the surface of the sea.

—Half-way Walking

I do not deserve these daughters for whom wind's
a word they name but cannot spell. They're all grace
notes, thyme bundles, while I've become the sandal-footed
      one,
returned from another realm, not of death exactly, but a new
      way
of bumping against things. It's no mere tale
that the night skies fill with horses. My daughters
gave me the story and I believe them.

—Pasiphae Invents Flamenco

This is body-as-beast.
I have no scripted smile
to reassure you. Watch
as I arch my back, face
downward, square shoulders
above dangling arms.
I can be a bull or its tamer.
My feet assert their own rhythms
as I face, feint, dodge.
Then arms entwine,
spiral up and *como la paloma*
I am a dove, fingers fluttering
from the tip of my frame.
I don't ask for help
but if you clap, sustain it.
Give me hands incessant
as the wind, and if you sing
make it not melody,
but cry. I want pure *grito*
from mouths formless
as despair. When you look at me
you will know you are looking
passion, or pain, in the eye.

iii.
Impressionable Earth

February Teacher

Like Ariadne with her thread
I pass our grated storefronts. Hopeful shingles
—Tonsorial Parlor, Nubian Patios—
blur by. The burden is great this month,
the skies lower. Three stout women with mops
stand at the door of the Temple
of Deliverance, bend to the cold, pat
their pockets for a key.

I can't avoid this catalog of signs:
these cubistic messages leap out at me
from gritty angular surfaces. Salt,
dried in the asphalt, crackles underfoot.
Today we talked about Thoreau
treading his path to the pond, and I know I mourn most
a loss of memory, how the buildings
sagged around this intersection, lock out
the impressionable earth.

I didn't do Henry justice today
but I was looking for you, and you'd driven on
with a laugh and a wave. It was last year
you ducked past me through the classroom door,
grinned and said, "I think I'm a Transcendentalist."
I'd never take in all this architecture
at once, perpendicular planes, boarded windows,
but I think how you'd take this same roadway

and stretch it as far as you could, into a straightaway,
the Harley between your knees purring,
echoing your not-so-nascent energies, drawing you
away from our fumes into mint and leather
on the wind. You'd cross open pastures
and wade waist deep in the waters of the mind

and I'd send you on, tanked up, ready to go.
It's my job, you see, to rethread the maze, again
and again, never minding the scenery,
or lack of it, one-way streets, dead-ending.

The story always repeats itself. You survive
the labyrinth. Of course you leave me behind.
Midsummer nights will find me, beached, alone,
not regretting, as I look up, hear you roar away,
and the stars bend to join me.

Reader Response

(after teaching Yusef Komunyakaa's "My Father's Love Letters" at Henry Ford High School, Detroit, Michigan)

His discussion group has figured it out:
the mother did the right thing
by taking her leave, no matter the child
she left behind. But McMaine holds firm,
determined to see it his way.
When they point out how the line breaks
at "happy," the child "somehow . . . happy"
the mother had gone, McMaine reads
right past the happiness. The sentence ends
with "gone"—a stronger tone which to him
means forever. Dead. The mother in the poem
didn't simply excuse herself from bruises, abuse,
didn't become the dish that ran away
dodging the fist that would send her—
"Pow!"—to the moon. Not that tired story.
For him it's a deeper tale: bones buried
beneath a tree the small bird's warning
warbles from, a song so threaded
through his days, eyes, breath, mind
every tree he passes sings it, every mother's absence
means forever. Gone. The page blank.
The book closed. So when he leans to his paper
full of erasures and empty
of the details I would coax from him,
I think how what the mother serves the child
dishes out, creating always the same
painstaking pattern: the plate beside the knife
between the fork and spoon. I watch as he writes
"What I remember about that day is
(here he fills in a date) *my first birthday*
(in fact, his tenth) *without her"*—and I know I'm reading
an emptiness that has surely become
his polestar, his fixed center, a leaping beast,
an absence forever present in his sky.

Waterworks

Behind his junkyard fence
the German shepherd noses
danger, paces past upended
barrows or fireblackened drums.
Each morning I pass him
at this crossroad. Evenings, nearby,
I walk my dachshund, a dog
not much larger than the teutonic
sneeze he sounds like. Our neighborhood
is full of dog, one incessantly maddened
by a nextdoor cat, all confined.
But say we let these furry
denizens leap their wire meshes.
Let them stream through the streets
and form a bounding river
of dogbacks. Let them join
the invisible hounds
that swirl around me and set
the fountains free. Doesn't everything
eventually achieve its level
of wildness, its half-life
of decay? Take the waterworks
my great grandfather penned and planned—
his 19th century draftsmanship now nets
loosened gratings and flaked metal
screens. But say we translate his Prussian
positivism into this doberman
or mastiff stalking stiffly down the street—
or transform our canine river
into a righteous corps of dogs—
won't generations of breeding
still squirm under the rusted fence,
their heavy haunches digging against
the dirt? Down there, where tunnels

signal habit, the gold bitch has escaped.
When will she return, her oblivious
tongue lolling, her tail
bright as a flag? Not so Pater Wilhelm
who died on my birthday
the year before I was born.
Bright, too, his white-winged moustache
and polished cheeks, his back snapped to
attention. He fled Bismarck's army
but still maintained such posture,
stern and staring in that photo I found,
although today his waterways follow
a different baton and the coy dolphins
intended strictly as design—
ornamental, peripheral figures—
the water channels through them now.
The edges of the fountain
have disappeared and the whole field's
flooded, the wild dream sloshing
about. What would my patronymic
forbear think? Illinois, Ohio,
probably even Michigan,
his realms of pipe and plumbing
steeped through filtered with lead
poisoning children and the most
orderly of folk averting
their eyes. No wonder I have trouble
sleeping. It takes self-
justification to dream simple
dreams. Yet there he was,
blind at the end of his days,
sweepingly optimistic, and heedless
as hell of this hecate daughter,
drafting and dodging her way
through these streets, unarmed
but followed by a stink of dogs,
their hot breath coating her calves.

Memorial Day Weekend

Along southbound I-75, recently planted trees
sway through a fog that smells
the way crackheads smell
who've been using too long.
Background blurs to foreground
and back again. Mugginess

saturates the spaces between us
until the very air quarrels with vision,
and here I'm the camera
without the film, trafficking from home
to market, everywhere the same.

At the Eastern Market I try to ignore
milky puddles oiled greenish-white,
merchants' scowls, peelings,
rinds, slippery and smeared. No relief,
not even from rain, as burglar alarms
are triggered by the damp.

When a day begins like this,
when resentments fester longer than I care to admit,
I'm not surprised to stand later,
near tears, looking out, listening
to wide drops of rain

dotting our magnolia's leaves,
the same tree I've tried six months
to avoid seeing ever since Andy,
our gentle friend, was shot dead
point blank in his home one block away.

I press my head against our door,
the new one, with the bars, installed
two days after the funeral, and recall that night, the tree
an ice-coated candelabra, illumined
in our neighbor's halogen security glare.

It seemed a new thing then to notice
how every single twig ended in a bud,
and I sensed in the tree a kind
of supplication, muted and glazed
beyond the reach of love.

I see no sense in looking
for cause or effect,
but it's not hard to understand why
all this time I've tried not to watch
as ice formed on the buds,

and the buds peeled back their velvet husks,
or petals later, before we swept them away,
layering the asphalt,
taking on waffle-like patterns
the color of blood or rust
from the soles of our shoes.

So Fast

(for Judy)

At seventy your mother was peppery,
ginger, pedaling her one-speed bike
through Maine's unharvested fields.
Her flowers spilled and spelled
the summer: yellow, white, asters
daisies. Grasses, too, and grain.

Today you have no time for the slow
embroideries of words. Only the clean
corners matter. "We could lose her
by Christmas. It's going so fast," you say.
She taught you the difference between sugar
and salt, stiff upper-lipping it
no matter the trial. Now, too late
for sweetness, you find yourself
seasoned the same. Fridays you rush
from work, gather your few things, drive
two states away to tend to her
and your father shuffling
through his despair, not quite sure what
will come next.
                          Family diplomat,
eldest daughter, I learn from you
loving constraints. How patiently
you take her last dictations,
record names and dates,
make notes and arrangements.
How feverishly in the early dark
they spill out of you, these poems
enclosed in the card you send
with its lupines and bluebells,
mother love and bitterness,
all in the same bouquet.

And Where Were the Foxes?

The nature center had closed
for the night when they walked
the marsh that harsh late spring
and circled on the boardwalk
nodding stretches of cattails,
frozen and thawed, sodden
from the weight of winter.
                It was then she learned
how childhoods erode to singular
terrains despite the constellations
we inherit, though then there were
no stars and where were the foxes,
the pouncing, yipping cubs
they searched for?
                Someone had seen them—
an alert and primal family—
but in that vespered twilight
no matter how they squinted across reeds
and bogs they saw only dabbling
ducks, not foxes, those warm bodies
likely curled under the exhausted
winter mat, deeply burrowed.

There was no opening or return
from their small centripetal selves,
nothing they would ever
comprehend, caught as they were
in husks they could not leave behind
as footfalls on the soggy, weathered
wood. It was the last conversation
with a brother she would not see again.
Wood ducks, seeking nests, shot
through trees, found branches, landed
farther on. Irrelevant trajectories.

At Silver Creek Presbyterian Church
(Lindale, Georgia 1953)

We tossed sticks from the bridge
that spanned the creek, my brother and I,
draped ourselves over iron railings,
or counted rings from stones we dropped
and we did not think about redemption.

The creek circled the church
and we crossed it Sundays to sit on pews
itching to run through tall grass
to the Confederate Soldier's grave
at wood's edge where the churchyard ended.

We'd flip through hymnals,
sing along with the simpler tunes
and just once was worship broken
by the songs of a Negro congregation
wading in the water.

I craned to see whole bodies
dressed in robes being dunked under,
heard only unaccompanied tongues,
a harmony from beneath the bridge
where we played our idle games.

It was baptism, full immersion
in a minor key, a vibration
crossing the yard, reaching
through open windows, filling us
with sound, and my body

trembling with resonance
at the suddenness of their joyful noise,
the stern nudge not to look,
to be still, sit polite
under the rafters of Our Lord.

Dixie, in Translation

(Atlanta, Georgia)

In tenth grade Latin, the whole class sang,
"Volum esse in terra gossypi."
It was "Dixie," in translation.

That was when Phoebe Puckett
danced the dirty boogie, as boys
threw coins at her in the darkened gym,

giving the girls choice news to chew on
behind their *Gallic Wars*, while Miss Lowe,
young and vibrant with the old certainties,

planned the annual slave banquet.
We rehearsed that land of cotton,
but what did we know, or care,

of the dark-skinned children
who walked to school swallowing
dust from passing buses,

whose parents took off their hats,
worked in our kitchens,
whose proper names we never knew?

We were dolls awaiting frilly dresses,
Kleenex crimped with bits of yarn, like Phoebe,
parading as Venus in her white sheet

the day before the banquet
while Earo ironed my new toga
in a corner of the room. Phoebe,

snickering by the window
—*"rhymes with zero!"*—at Earo's name,
and me smirking at her side.

Redlipped Phoebe, I wanted her to teach me
how to walk the runway, steal the show.
I wish I'd had the heart to resist

her laughter crisp as the percale
drape she wore. Eager to claim
my freshman slave, bid him peel,

then pop, grape after grape into
my open mouth, I was ignorant
of Earo that fall afternoon. Earo,

who came to us on Thursdays to press
our common clothes. Earo, who spoke little
but said once, *"A change is gonna come,"*

with a voice that tells me now
all the percale in the world, all the chenille
hanging from pines along back roads

or smoothed by ivory hands
will never obscure the burlap bags
so rough to drag a baby on

along those rows of knife-edged
plants, never cover the taproot, fiber
and seed of it. No matter

how many azalea blossoms layer
the spring woods, then fall passively to earth
she must have known some new song

would rise to unwind our refrain
and rend that false fabric, cut through
the merciless air.

Letter From Atlanta

Two saffron-headed parrots
in a dark, three-story cage replicate
the logo of the Hyatt chain. At night
their cries sound throughout the atrium
in this convention center a century
of layers above streets Sherman burned.

The town we knew has been redone
in girders and glass—so in our old yard
I tried not to be surprised, but Tom,
the woods are so overgrown I'd never find
that toy house you buried, graves
of pets, our childhood offerings.

I guessed how long a magnolia took
to thrust through cement at the patio's edge,
or when these pines, tinder dry, fell crosswise
over other trees, but who could gauge boarded
windows, frat-house graffiti, beery lines
of hula dancers shimmying on our walls?

Feet snarled in vines, my mind a tangle
of half-recognitions, the children who gazed
up through windows listening for bells
felt barely familiar or dreamed. Last night
I met a woman who fled to the North
and came to tell of terror with grace and love.

As we parted I craned to see her
ride the lighted capsule, smiling,
ten floors up. How odd it seemed—
the same stretch to my neck
as earlier that day, at the edge of our wood,
I watched a broadwing lift above the trees.

In the North Country

A hawk drops behind me, slicing down
on drumbeat wings. I can't see it. I only
feel the predatory swath, lightning-like,
as if the air itself opens, then closes
and the day, the prey and I, waist high
in sun and tall grass, all suddenly change.

Then, another wilderness exchange
as on a marshy trail my niece kneels down
to find the exact spot between high
weeds and wingbeats so that with only
a single breath she snatches and closes
her hand around a dragonfly. How I like

her move! The day brightens and swirls like
ether around her. I think she knows change
without knowing it. Her gesture closes
and telescopes my history down
like a camper's cup, collapsible, only
rarely used for drinking, normally stored high

on a shelf. But now a shining buzz high-
lights my thirst for an energy, like
that insect's after-image: feral, lonely,
less dispassionate. When will my pulse change,
become more impulsive? My gaze drops down.
Her hand flies open, then quietly closes.

It's flown. The dry scratch in my throat closes
on spidery legs my brother found high
under the eaves of childhood, brought down
to chase me into foolishness like
the southern girls I tried not to be. Change
brings hope, not for a new order only,

but pure disregard. Let memory only
last the briefest while. What the heart loses
reappears in pearly water, puddles changed
to mirrors on the path or the high
flight of the now-free dragonfly. Business-like,
my girl brushes her hands, smooths her hair down.

She faces her father, my only brother, with high
pride, my small priestess, who discloses all like-
nesses of change the moment she pulls the insect down.

A Bad Day For Bees

they told us in the ER, as if
I had not already felt in your wrist
nothing but my own rapid-fire heart
as I dashed about, checking, touching you,
dialing EMS, fetching ice, just for God's sake not
stopping, as if each second-by-second
move would surely bring you back
from wherever the venom had taken you.
You'd had shutters to paint, a lawn
to mow, when the insect's sting
sent you stumbling up the stairs,
and the stream you urinated then
seemed nearly endless until you slumped
senseless against the cold tiles and I
couldn't find your pulse. Except for you,
nothing was holding still that day
and I paced the waiting room,
seeking some tough nurselike savvy,
something to come between me and my
quaking, my making too much of manic
cartoons on the monitors, or hissing doors.
At your bedside at last, remarks from beyond
the mobile curtain *("while you're still well enough,*
while you still have time") made echoes
I tried not to hear. *"Anaphylactic shock,"*
they said—the way the body buffers itself.
Yes, I thought. That's good, a buffer, like time,
a reprieve, something ludicrous—like you
snapping at medics, cranky with everyone—
and me thinking helplessly of our old dog,
his jaws clacking happily, snapping
after yellow jackets. I swear
he'd have gotten that bee, us egging him on,
speculating at the buzz it gave him.

62

How These Landscapes Dwarf Us

It's as if we're standing on some distant cliff
scanning a dim horizon.
In the gorge below a torrent rushes.
Then sun dissolves the mist and there they are:
the capsized boat, its tiny passengers
we watch—but cannot warn—hurtling toward falls

they cannot see. Or it's how, in the photograph
by Edward Curtis, the Pueblo potter
reverses figure, ground. Back toward the camera,
shawl gusting up from the fire at her feet,
she looks away, to some vanishing point,
forms a dark window against the sky.

Easy these days to drift into landscapes
and get lost searching what's beyond the frame.
Better restrict our view, like peasants
in Zen scrolls who occupy corners, take up
less space than a bush, prod diminutive
donkeys along ledges in the foreground.

It's our last talk, a dim winter's day.
"Go to Paris," you say. "Find the Japanese
exhibits. Those human figures—how small
they are." Last trip there, you wore a beret,
delighted to be asked to give directions.

Now, like Boddhisatva on his turtle,
robes flowing, eyes fierce and clear,
you direct me to scrutinize brush strokes,
observe "the quick ink," your silvery hair
finally grown back in, spilling, billowing out
as if caught by what mountain wind.

Twilight Body and Field

i.

I refuse to harvest
this news of illness
floating through your veins

and I cannot see you there
sliced, stitched, stunned
by the doctors' verdict.

Write *you* off? Never.
It is late summer. Tomatoes
burst from vines, kernels

of corn swell with milk,
and now these fields
bending to a twilight

that makes ears of wheat
seem lit from within.
Is it consolation

to see vision as a gift
not given to forcing
in lucent bodies of grain?

What brings us closer
than the earth I do not know
except the growing world

somehow becomes our story
and we speak from this
together as we breathe.

ii.

Like the missing limb
in the *Pietà* my dream
lingers, phantom pain.

I have not wept at your news
and when I explain
find only the obvious—

the number of hours
under the knife, a numbing
sentence of time.

I think of Christ's arm
buried in folds of cloth
or stone, absent yet implied.

It was nothing you said
but the way I dreamed
I held you wakened me:

your body naked,
turning away, hugely white,
facing forward like a son.

Voyager

Fireflies map the edges of trees,
chart deciduous shapes
backlit by a wash of stars.

On-and-off blinkings. A tree is,
is not. Greens turn black in this light
and we become water looking up

into a well where we could drown.
Father, I would drown in your
forgiveness. Tender to me this hope,

this vowel, liquid and round.
When we were children your arms
embraced us, the hairs we stroked,

comforting pelt. Arm smooth
as marble, hairless, disentangled;
arm I take to guide you

across the lot to your car.
Through the humid night
comes music, Holst's *Planets*—

Jupiter? Or Mars? Revolutions
of strings, racing bows. The chords
stop us. Where are we going?

You've lost night vision, you tell me.
Stars blur. You confuse alleys, driveways,
do little of the driving now.

Uncertain, your foot reaches
where a step is not,
wavers to an off beat. If only

I could alter this awkward
syncopation and, sostenuto,
help you find the ground.

I hold your arm, as I hold you
to the next step, to the planet
receding beneath your feet.

iv.

The Work of Her Hands

Walking Stick

Think of it as captured lightning—
something that will keep you
connected to the earth. Select it

from the stand of the folk artist
whose hands brought forth
the textured vein. She has others

less smooth, of course—an inverted
root clump, now a truncated Medusa,
each snaky face painted

in a loopy smile—or the sumac stick,
brass-tipped, ridged and knobbed
like a gnawed corncob. Some say

the wood tells her what to find,
or else it's her hickory hands
giving her vision. Her glance

strikes stump or twisted vine
before she pares to the essential
eye, tooth, scale, claw, fang.

Under her blade, knots bulge,
breathe. Birds take wing. Surely
the whole forest is awake to her.

The boards of our houses
swell when she passes, like seas
to the moon, tide beneath bark.

Even in chopped and muted blocks
drops of sap find surface, whorls speak
and interrupt the grain.

Letter Perfect

Say *"ah"* for pottery.
For poetry say *"oh."*

The letters don't hold still,
the t's switch with the e,
and I'm in the mix again

sinking my fingers
into the slip, that blend
of earth and water

like blood or gravy
that eases the friction
between hand and clay.

Later I learned a new word
for it, *slurry*, and though
that potter is dead now

still the word becomes
his shy, burry voice
and quick, skilled hands.

He taught me to trust
both slippage and speed,
to ride the wet slur

and hold on tight,
pressing the opening
oblivious to flyings-off.

You pull and turn,
pushing outward and in,
till at last the form appears

the spun circle: ready
to set and take to the fire,
to turn molten, cool

then still, ringing
its perfect empty **O**.

Anasazi Bowl

She who takes down the bowl
listens through funereal
holes for the sigh of a maker,

seepage from a mortal
body. Around the inner rim
of fine micaceous clay

Anasazi lightning—ancient
and contained—flickers
then fades against the real

mountains that flash when rain
releases fragrance from dust
and gives her godlike breath.

It's the work of her hands—
or it could be—not hers
but another she who—

Who? Wind in the canyon. Ravens
tumbling through air. She looks
into this world her hands

hold not as spirit lost
but roundness and what remains
fragile   the singing clay.

In Taos, New Mexico

*—upon learning, after visiting Kit Carson's House, how
Kit traditionally gave Mrs. Carson a bolt of the finest silk
after the birth of each of his eight legitimate children.*

Lace conceals our senora on the stair
but an unscreened window reveals
the view. The mountain makes
you think it can move.

An unscreened window reveals
the roof of Kit Carson's House.
You think it can move?
Anywhere you are, you are a tourist.

The roof of Kit Carson's House—
you see, it's a shining thing.
Anywhere you are, you are a tourist.
In the grasses a hummingbird passes

you. See, it's a shining thing,
silvery, like wooden crosses
in the grasses. Watch as it hums and passes
suddenly, in a vanishing line,

the silvery wooden crosses—
how it becomes a trace of itself,
a suddenly vanishing line.
Kit Carson's Indian wife

became a trace of herself—
Singing Rain, her Arapahoe name.
Kit Carson's Indian wife
was not the one who was named

(Singing Rain, her Arapahoe name)
not in this display. Her children forgotten,
she was not the one who was named,
not the one given silk

in this display. Her children forgotten,
she finds no place here, she who was
not the one given silk,
who gave no legitimate birth for his name.

Who gave no legitimate birth, how did she view
the view the mountain makes,
she, who finds no place here, where
lace conceals her shadow on the stair?

Anonymous Northwest Coast Indian Painting

No boundary or horizon here: each
square inch within the frame is dedicated
to an ancient, up-front
animal design, or a series of them
                              as one shape shifts
into another like cuneiform dreams,
animal dreams, feathers becoming
paddles or the rattles whale hunters dreamed
to turn the beast successfully
                         toward shore;
                         but this is not subliminal, no,
rather *liminal*, as in threshold, doorway
the art of Tlingit or Haida
to make their homes
              welcoming spaces, framed
by motifs or stories growing in and out
of one another. On totem poles
Bear disgorges Frog who holds
a small man in his belly:
                    so what's human here
may be exactly the way Beaver's eyes
suggest palms or paws, or how Bear's teeth
glaring from the center could be
the grillwork of a shiny car or a birth canal,
                    a door opening
out or in, no matter. Raven
holds down the corners while
in the middle Bear
                    dominates, his eyes
like small ravens, the same
foetal forms, figures
that become ground as we

          squint and stare and Bear

and Beaver merge, hatched lines take up
red, then blue, now here a fin
looks like a fluke and I get lost
following the reason of it.

Some things may be too strong
to see or understand, my son says
centering the picture over the door
in his new apartment
                    as I think of orchids

                    or mountains,
how what's small or large
can overwhelm equally, while outside all
of Seattle throbs, shouts, barks
and enters too: Hare Krishna
chants from the room downstairs,
footsteps from the one above:
                    the floor's another
threshold, and the windows and our ears:
surfaces that pulse as we wait
for the strange to become familiar
a whole woodland watching as

                    tsa! tsa! CrowDancer
                    or Raven lands, both feet at once,
                    low to the ground, arms awhirl
                    and jumps like that, two-footed, again
                    and again, his costume dangles clicking
                    a whitenoise hiss up into hemlock branches,
                    fir, light rising through them, this

all-at-onceness, memory,
dreams, jumping forward in these
eyes, eyes of cedar and frog,
eyes of the forest, eyes of the past
revealing no stories but letting,
I like to think, everything in.

At the Moscow Circus

the dancing bears catch rings with their paws.
Like a sluggish man this one sways, seems at a loss
as rings cascade through the air and form
a rippling sheath along his arm.

The illusion comes and goes and I don't deny
I almost see them as "real"—all of them, the bear
inside the man inside the bear. Where
does it end? Tigers melt through their hoops. Horses
like these have outrun wolves, pulled troikas
through the hardest cold and yes, the well-arched neck's
a sign of excellent training, but that cossack
dangling alongside the galloping hooves, is
he master of the beast or just drunk with wildness
for some lost Ninotchka?
Surely the rider has his sorrows—but so did my Turkish
friend, on her way from Istanbul to New York,
who, without a word of Russian (and tanked on vodka,
misery and love) found a driver to find the grave
where her exiled countryman Hikmet lay.
As if all it took to get her there was the name—
Hikmet—a name like a talisman, an arrow
through those dark confusing streets,
leading her at last to the one man in all of Moscow
who would take her there, where she could weep
for her poet and laugh and wail, pounding the ground
till well past midnight before the plane carried her on.
Oh comrades, think of internationalism at its best—one
human heart in time with another, one clown
masking his sorrow, one dazed terpsichorean
bear, or poet. The spangles are nothing.
Artistry is dangerous, with or without a net. Clutching
our popcorn, flashing lightswords into the dark,
we stare transfixed. The tightrope walker

in his burlap hood could be death himself crossing that wire,
balancing his pole, each foot gripping steadily forward,
the human shape within the bag stretching blindly,
inching along, making it look so easy,
coming toward us, whether or not we know.

After "The Death of Cleopatra" by Edmonia Lewis

Long after her own death the sculptor appears
in the journal of African-American artists,
the one with the roses on the cover
paying delicate, pastel homage to
those 19th century unenslaved Americans
becoming/being their art despite an oppression
one shrinks to imagine—and hers, the mysterious
Edmonia who stares from the daguerreotype
shawl-draped waist, cocked hat, stubborn chin.
Her Cleopatra eyes give nothing of the story
and why should we deserve it? It is not my tale
to tell, only to trace a courage, stitch a pattern
of determination, the way she embroidered her life,
created her own queen, gave her best to abolition
then left false trails of stories behind.

She was probably not wigwam-born, Ojibway-raised
as she would have them have it, a persona invented
to tweak dull fears, but the record remains
how she was dragged from her lodgings, accused
of poisoning a white girl, fellow student, beaten,
luckily not killed in Oberlin, Ohio
from where she fled to an upper atelier in Rome
looking out over rooftops, flowerpots.
Frederick Douglass found her there, contented and busy
with sculpting, studies, plans.

Who can feature the horror in the night and who
would want to, but it must have marked her so
that every gesture she would make from then on
would arrive in a marble so pure, so ethereal,
it would exceed any other purity, would become
a rhythm of defiance, purity of icy nights

and the great starry path of the ancestors
carrying truths from a forest deep and primeval enough
to disappear in, to hide, fly away through a darkness
that would lift above kerosene-spattered mud-churned
          roadways
rude hands dragging her, voices accusing—*poison*?

If anything her sculptures became more scrupulous,
became weapons rabble could never recognize,
and resistance now is what we read in the collapsed
body of the queen, the bad weather of centuries
surpassed by the sculptor's chiseling even in death
a woman's power. Chin raised against the mob,
accused poisoner, with "Cleopatra"
she turns it all inside out, the poison a choice now—
oh Isis, mother of dawn, mother of rivers
who gives her this garland of strength and mantle of twins
to drape her relief—not a whore, not Antony's plaything,
she leans back, full of force and death
                              into her gleaming

white refutation.

The Blues, "The Bay"
(after Helen Frankenthaler)

The bay fills the canvas
a cerulean spill shifting into aquamarine,
the blues thicker in places where the artist's squeegee
scraped across the surface and piled pigment onto
                                        itself.
Eleven shades of blue, iris and
gentian blue steeped like an infusion
of petals in water—a violet turning
cobalt blue, electric blue.

I think how blues can build until suddenly
you've got some subterranean smoky form of them
—Capital B blues, Memphis Blues, my very own blues—
but it's the edges interest me—
the interdigitation of these fine
fingers of paint where boundaries
clasp like hands or furrow into fjords
from landscapes I've often dreamed.

And I love this primary culture
clash, the seepage of one color into
another, the fungal, organic fringe
of whatever pulses across a petri dish,
swells magma upward or defines the throbbing
voice of a crowd, the contours of a continent.

So here's lower India, swathed in blue
being swallowed in a wash of green—
or is its cloudlike wedge about to overrun
this patience of marsh, verdure, grass?

And what to make of the crisp swatch of taupe?
Or the wry central fillip of burnt Sienna
but a wisp, a swipe of a smile?

Hard to tell, to find the form in formlessness,
and under it all, the canvas, raw, enticing focus.
Here: this one bare slit seems to let in light
like the eye of the painter, an invitation to peer through
from the other side.

Still Life With Migraine

(Contemplating the pomegranate in Van Eyck's "St. Jerome
in His Study")

Washed red in the light trembling
against the walls of the saint's
mahogany chamber, and bathed vermilion

in the arrangement of his cape, his brassbound
box, his mind—but I am not poised
like the saint, nor patient as the lion

curled and dreaming at his feet. More like
my own hound, exhaling in sleep
her unconscious woofs, paws twitching

as if some spark touched a chain of nerves.
I will put this print aside.
I will add new strokes to the dark

apple of my migraine lest the paint dry
fixing me forever. Here all I see is jaggedly
bright. Peripheries dance and snap.

In the kitchen plumbing drips and whispers.
A neon-white horsehair snakes across my vision
fluid as memory, and as globed

as the fruit I peeled and painted,
years ago, lodged behind my eyes now,
like a poem, or a grenade.

To accept the pomegranate is to remember
the first death, a burst of sorrow
on a bright fall day. It's twenty-nine years

since I opened that mail and still
one letter bleeds into another—that mail,
that news, and how weeping then

I went farther back—and saw myself,
aged nine, skinny, pigtailed, unaware,
when my mother's friend called me

to her steaming tub, bade me
touch her naked belly as the baby
moved beneath her skin.

Astonished, embarrassed, I wanted to run,
but now I see her roundness and feel
the stretched hide, the light shield shining.

There is no heart to the pomegranate,
a fruit without a core. Beneath the gloss
of Van Eyck's egg tempera patina, placed

just so atop the jar of snakebite antidote—
the orb only stands for our struggle,
each dihedral seed in its ruby red cell

bearing ransom from oblivion, brittle
promise from the realm of darkness—
as if a swap of seeds could answer
the death of any daughter.

Indonesian Puppet Doll

If not the muse, it surely was my friend
sent this present to my outstretched arms
when I involuntarily opened them.
Unseeing, tuned to some inner alarm,
I reached without knowing I was reaching.
And what third eye, third ear had seen or heard
I can't say. The shop was full of I-Ching
charms, scents, soaps, Tibetan chimes; the cupboard
where I stood perusing linen dresses
so tall its topmost shelf almost concealed
its wares. Now all I have are guesses
at what I must have jarred, what was revealed.
I did not look. I merely sensed the fall,
stretched out my arms and there it was: the doll.

I stretched my arms and there it was, the doll
I saw as spirit sent. It's Toi, I said,
who'd left, yet still walked so much with me. All
day we'd talked of poems, wept, distracted
and now I stood shifting my weight before
this rack of dresses in sheer disbelief
at what I'd caught. I bought it, left the store
wondering at the angles of her grief
and if the flight path leading her away
inclined the same as the descent, the brisk
tumble of doll I had in my quiet way
protected. This catching—was it risk
or knowledge? Puppet, stand-in for myself,
I took it home and placed it on the shelf.

I took her home and placed her on the shelf
adjacent to Sophia's gorgeous "Queens"—
three bawdy colleagues in collage who dwell
against a heartstrewn tapestry of reds and greens.

They signal from their frame and she returns
her cool replies. They're bold, a birthday cake,
outburst of waving arms; each hand burns
corolla-like as if their bodies make
a single crown. I like to think Sophia, Toi
and I form one smooth line through this acclaim
entwining grief and surprise, art and joy.
Where one begins one ends, so arm in arm
we're kindred, looped like a moebius whose
turns reveal our friends, if not the muse.

v.
Clearing the Bird

The Santa Fe Crow

Casual east of the Rockies,
here this species of crow spreads
caw and cacophony over mall
and highway and now one clasps
stubbornly to the wire
above the adobe wall outside,
not moving despite the frantic dog
below it, so unmoving in fact
it's as if it takes some perverse
Poe-like pleasure
in the terrier's leaping
torque, the futile, four-legged spring
and ceaseless yap that try
again and again to dislodge the bird
but only succeed in pulling me
away from the piano, a score
I haven't tried in years, to rush
into the yard and hush the dog, shoo
the crow with almost the same "No!"
my mother used to call out from the kitchen
during practice as I stumbled
through the notes, disturbing her ear
tuned to a perfection I'd never know,
only here I am again trying
to get it right: the tone, the key,
the arcing line that shapes the phrase,
to sort the jumbled chord
knotted above the stave, its top line
like the wire crow lifts from
as it downflaps, just once, a split
second there I can almost see
my errant notes take shape,
bearing their mistaken half-tones
from the bench in the living room

over to her stove where they hover
above casserole or spaghetti,
the utter wrongness of them
must have made her windowless kitchen
feel even narrower, tighter, a sharp
I'd flattened, a flat I'd forgotten, a joy
diminished, remembered today in
its absence as crow
shakes its shawl of shadow
like a dancer tossing fringe about her,
the feathers edging me where I will
not willingly go.

Blackbird Memoriam, November 1995

What keeper loosed this swarm?
Blackbirds fill the air, form like bees
or thick black spots, a cloud of oily dots.
They flow as one large cell, to shrink
or swell until the magnet breaks, the bonds
dissolve and each one lands on the nearest branch
to sit, rise at the next cue.

               A continent away,
Nigeria today puts all sky in question.
Its branches hold the nine newest victims.
Martyrs, dangling, they will not rise.

               With migrant flocks
autumn's darkening hour reminds:
whatever force brings thousands of starlings
to one fantastic form cannot prevent this harm
from poisoning the innocence of birds.

               And yet I'd let these words
take a different wing, if not to fly
then sing, or if no voice be found
above that killing ground, whisper then
forbidden prayer that hope long hidden
issue forth, promising from heart or earth
antidote to sorrow.
            Ken Saro-Wiwa—courage for tomorrow.

Ars Poetica: Clearing the Bird

To pry open panic's jaws, we've come.
To free them from the frantic pockets they've made.
To untangle terror from feather and claw and lift
them out of the nets we've set, sending them up to air again.
To be left behind where we stand,
boots deep in swampy ground.

To extract the bird requires knowing
the exact angle of entrance, finding the way
the tangle was made, so we hold it up and look
for the clear spot above the heart
before clasping the head with our fingers,
body cupped in our palm.

Then the pencil, dull point best,
with which we pick and pull the hairlike
strands of twine, invisible
to a bird in flight, now knotted into webs
of warbler, thrush, and wren, densely wrapped,
wings worst to remove.

Over the shoulder, under the chin
we lift the net one thread, one feather
at a time. Sometimes they struggle against us.
Sometimes a head's so snarled
we fear we'll yank it off in the last stretch of line
over the open beak.

And we want to move quickly, not stressing the bird,
quickly, lest it overheat in the sun
and the blue film of defeat spread across its eye.
How clumsy we feel. Our haste itself
slows us as we try not to think, let
fingers work without us—

method take control. Our pencils stir and lift
the threads and the bird's our only focus.
We don't notice the willows around us,
and this song we sing, as if to an infant,
must be for ourselves, to calm us as we work
to free the hotblooded form.

For My Sister

You thought the pewee only raised one brood
but the heavy boat you knocked down from the eaves
unanchoring its keel of plastered mud
held five new eggs. Below the dappled leaves
they shone like pearls, their tapered shapes begging
to be touched. But who'd expect detachment
would bear such awful stink? I rushed, gagging,
for a hose, soap, the sink. A wretched scent
its gloss, the emerald nest was threaded
with grass, moss, your guilt. Unintentional,
I said, no worse than any snake's wedged head
slithering toward a fledgling: a natural,
if cold-blooded, comfort. The pewee's clock's
reset by now. Feathers fall. Cradles rock.

On Hearing the Songs of Wolves as Mirrors of Desire
(for Kristin)

In northern Minnesota
some tourists from Arizona
stand under a winter sky.
Their guide lets forth an eerie
string of notes and suddenly
the whole bowl of the heavens
spills over with sound.
              They're out there—
wolves among the trees, pacing
then pausing to answer this human
imitation of their kind.
How easily the guide lures them
to his purpose, not as pelts or trap-
bitten paws, but performance wolves:
habitat invaded, money exchanged.

Exhaust fumes from the bus cross
the crusted snow, yet surely
the tourists stamping for warmth
beneath that starry resonance
shiver less from cold than a hunger
to call, and respond—and be
responded to—by the glittering,
hair-raising dark
                  just as we,
in our kitchens, where the radio
brings the story, feel our napes prickle
as we set down a napkin
or put back a fork and look up
to let an echoing sky
fill our mind's eye, a multitude
of wolf tongues dancing in our ears
as if some wild cosmic composer
set the aurora borealis to music.

97

Eleven Herons

What's flapping through the air is equalled
on the shore, though two of us aren't here—

girl cousins, playing tricks at sunset, flaunting
the hilarious power of their absence.

The approaching flock's almost overhead
when it swerves east, into the oncoming dark,

revealing, by ragged flight, not geese,
perfectly V-ed, but Great Blues, eleven of them,

just as we are eleven, siblings with children,
the adults counting in amazement at what flies

toward the trees. As if with one will,
the flock. As if with one soul, the family.

But where are Betsy & Olivia, hiding
in the dunes, rustling bushes like small birds?

No calls flush them. Nothing replies but the sky's
deepening reds as we wait for the flash of green

that signals the sun's drop below the water.
Agents of farewell, my sister says, of the vanishing

birds—or girls—while I wonder what secret door
they found, what passage to enchantment

here at twilight, where fact and legend
threaten to cross. Although a rookery's

the birds' destination—its platforms
of twig & branch limed with excremental

whitewash & feathered stink—it still belongs
in a black forest. Bored now, my nieces

file down the dune, wrap up in towels,
brush off the immutable sand—while I turn

to view headlands made vague by mist
as if the lake gives back to the air

some part of itself, as magenta & orange
spread like oil on water and above us

cirrus swirls spin a loose, open fan
of feathers or fringe, heron wings, string

of words to place against the sky.

Calling the Owl

This time the owl eludes us
where we stand trying to call him in
                          with his own voice
which we've captured on tape
to release to the predawn woods.

Press a button. The air flutters,
rushing from our black box
                          what is hidden from us—
wing-like quaverings—
                soft bursts of song.

If light mutes him, shadows offer hope,
and we listen so intently into them
                          the snowy meadow
suddenly seems wider, brighter
with news from beyond its perimeter.

Don't lift, I almost pray,
                          don't disappear.
Day will break soon enough.
Let us hear your faint vibrato and absorb
what is invisible, wild and nearly gone.

Mist thickens the silence, promises
patience, echo, sound not sight.
I will let that fluty tremolo find,
                          fill me, give voice
to emptiness. I hold my breath to sustain
                the long vowel of night.

On the Mockingbird Singing in the Morning in the Barrio a Few Blocks from the Boardwalk on the Beach in Venice, California

Above the bougainvillea, coming unstuck
from this stuccoed urban maze,
a mockingbird is doing the best he can
to make something from the nothing
that precedes him. The voice
climbs, tumbles, and I wonder
if he is riding or falling from
the edge of his song,
this song he doesn't own
just as a surfer's not master
of the wave, no matter
the moves. Mock soloist,
our bird creates his own company.
He's a manic one-man birdband
conducting himself in early morning excess
beyond the hanging fuchsia
whose ruby silence
is preferable, perhaps,
to his cacophony—
but he's at it again now, letting go
or hanging on, his wheezing
takeoff like a whip
snapping, a carnival
toy to twirl in the air—
and in fact he rises, up for a moment,
whirligig, wings a-windup,
then back to the branch
and his aphoristic repetitions,
the song gone a bit obsessive
and bizarre. And we who
grouse at his intrusions
blinking from sleep ruffled

for all we know by the latest passing
boombox—what else to do
but love the wild
array of him, how he tunes
himself up and gets it all
in, this fly-right-up clown, with his
step-right-up patter, saying
towhee and titmouse, meaning meadow
and glen, whatever it is, shape it,
take it, to what (*to-whee!*) to what is given.

Slipstream

We made a small parade, you and I—
temporary tenants of the sand,
Lake Erie flat beside us.
We did not speak but stepped along
to a solid rhythm, a method
I chose almost by chance—
to follow your footsteps
back from Fish Point, making sure
my feet fell exactly
into the imprints yours left behind.
This way of walking
conserved, I decided, energy,
and I'd hop now and then to match
my stride to yours:
left right i you
        right left you me.
A good mile or more of this
replication, and if our trail
wandered into non-waves,
little laplets from the lake
that loomed and simmered,
it was not a pot about to boil
but silky and peaceful as sand.
Head down, your heels all I could see
from beneath my hat's brim,
I may have missed what could have been
an eagle flying above the beach.
So what makes me love this mechanical
movement of one foot (mine)
into the space another's
(yours) seconds before evacuated?
Steady, yes, but unremarkable
as sweat sliding beneath my breasts
and I found myself missing

that eagle whistle. I imagined it
all the way back to car and cottage
thinking how some days our daily
goings-on seem so plain, regular,
no wind to rustle up waves,
nothing louder than sand
dropping its separate grains
beneath your lifting soles.

Once I thought if I didn't look
at what I wrote I could proceed
without thinking. Writing blind.
One word, then the next,
the way I look only at your tracks
and your tracks make one
unending sentence and we are
parallel with nothing
except the lake and what
does the lake dream
on days like this? Must
tranquillity always suggest
its opposite, or apposite?
Water, that looming
surface, and what's
a synonym for loom
except portend? Is there
a synonym for lake?
Water has no... I am
a synonym for...? Or
are you a...? No words
are exactly alike, I tell my students,
but we can synchronize, breathe
in tandem, in and out and in
step our feet almost in apposition,
or opposition, to one another.
I am a stand-in not for
you certainly whose energy

I think I am taking advantage of,
slipstreaming behind you,
neither of us carrying the other
though like that stock tale, the one
you find framed in card shops,
we left only one set of prints behind.
So which of us was a god and which
a burden and what's more sacred anyway
than our bodies in their ceaseless
pause pace skip pace pause?

What's the synonym for *thesaurus*
my student wanted to know,
so I told her there is no
synonym for "what."
We can't see substitutes
for shadows and there was
no hint of the eagle I thought I saw
but if I keep walking enough,
stalking, humming excuses like songs
about how I'm *"using you, sweet baby,*
till I use you up," perhaps I won't
remember what I missed, shiver of wings,
piercing whistle shaman rattle.
We look up think bird then it's gone
that opportunity for wonder. *Slipstream*:
a sound so lovely and so unlike
the vulture that perched
on the roof of the lecture hall
and floated every day
past four floors of mirrored windows—
not that aimless dark reflection, but a word
like a whisper, a way of spacing the air, of being
pulled or pulling, of migrating
and coming home.

Notes

p. 39 "Pasiphae: What She Wanted"

Pasiphae, queen of Crete, became mother of the Minotaur after consummating her lust for the bull from the sea—a punishment inflicted through her upon her husband, King Minos, who had greatly offended the god Poseidon.

"sandal-footed one:" a reference to "monosandalism," a recurring motif in IndoEuropean folklore. Individuals who entered the underworld and returned were said thereafter to wear one sandal or to walk with a limp.

"Pasiphae Invents Flamenco:" In pre-Athenian Cretan religion, Pasiphae was a goddess, daughter of the sun and the moon, and the bull was her sacred creature. Her cult was said to have spread to Spain.

p. 63 "How These Landscapes Dwarf Us"
p. 64 "Twilight Body and Field"

Written in memory of Lawrence Pike, 1932–95.

p. 71 "Walking Stick"

This poem is based upon a documentary aired on public television in the spring of 1991 featuring African-American women folk artists.

p. 81 "After 'The Death of Cleopatra' by Edmonia Lewis"

Information about Edmonia Lewis is taken from *The International Review of African American Art*, vol. 12, number 2, 1995 published by the Hampton University Museum.

p. 85 "Still Life With Migraine"

Written in memory of Kit Thoburn, 1954–62.

About the Author

Terry Blackhawk is the author of *Trio: Voices from the Myths*, a chapbook of poems from Ridgeway Press. Her poetry has appeared in many journals and has received numerous awards, including the 1990 Foley Poetry Award, a Distinguished Merit Award from PoetryAtlanta and finalist for the 1997 Marlboro Prize and the 1996 Four Way Books Intro Series competition. A former teacher with the Detroit Public Schools, she currently directs InsideOut, a writers-in-schools program which she founded in 1995 for Detroit youth. She was named a National Scholastic Writing Teacher in 1989 and the Michigan Creative Writing Teacher of the Year in 1990. She also received the 1994 United Black Artists Award for Pioneering Teacher in the Arts, an NBC Residency to teach writing from the classics, and a National Endowment for the Humanities Teacher-Scholar Sabbatical Award to study the work of Emily Dickinson. She has taught at Oakland University, Olivet College and Madonna University and has given writing workshops for the Detroit Institute of Arts and the Michigan Youth Arts Festival.

Terry Blackhawk was born in California, graduated Antioch College in the late 1960s and has lived in Detroit with her husband Evan most of her adult life. She received a masters degree from Wayne State and a Ph.D. in language arts education from Oakland University.